Thank

I want to say Thank You for buying my book, so I've put together a free gift for you!

More Awesome Dessert Recipes For Free

These additional recipes are the perfect complement to all the excellent recipes already in this book, and can be found at the website below:

http://www.kjjepublishing.com/almondflourbonus

Introduction

What is Almond Flour? 6

Benefits of Almond Flour & Almonds 6

Concerns with Almond Flour.. 7

Breakfast Recipes

Waffles with Cinnamon 9

Golden Blueberry Muffins 10

Fluffy Buttermilk Pancakes 12

Buttery Butter Biscuits 13

Tasty Oatmeal Raisin Bars 15

Cinnamon Vanilla Banana Bread... 17

Moist Pumpkin Spice Bread.. 19

Lunch Recipes

Great Green Bean and Almond Soup 22

Crispy Homemade Pizza Crust.. 24

Tasty Lean Beef Hamburgers 26

Juicy Turkey Burgers 28

Lip Smacking BBQ Buffalo Chicken Wings................................. 30

Chicken Tenders with Homemade Honey Mustard Sauce 32

Crispy Fish Sticks with Homemade Tartar Sauce...................... 34

Dinner Recipes

Satisfying Baked Hamburger Casserole with Cheese 37

Hearty Baked Turkey Meatloaf 39

Almond and Cheesy Parmesan Baked Fish 41

Tantalizing Turkey Meatballs 42

Savory Curry Chicken... 44

Heart Healthy Almond Crusted Salmon 46

(Oven-Fried) Fried Chicken 48

Creamy Fettuccine Alfredo with Almond Crusted Chicken 50

Dessert Recipes

Classic Chocolate Chip Cookies... 53

Scrumptious Apple Pie 55

Delectable Double Chocolate Brownies.................................... 57

Perfect Peanut Butter Cookies 59

Mouth-Watering Peach Crisp.. 61

Awesome Almond Brownies 63

Conclusion

Free Almond Flour & Almond Educational Resources............... 67

Shopping Resources 67

Introduction

Have you struggled to reduce your blood sugar after being advised by your doctor? Does it feel like you have headaches more frequently than you should? Or have acid reflux frequently? How about just wanting to "feel better" in general?

Removing wheat from your diet can be a healthy step for many of us towards these goals, and I congratulate you for taking the initiative to purchase this book, well done.

It's been written to fill a need for hearty, satisfying recipes that don't use grains such as wheat, barley, rye or triticale (a cross between wheat and rye). You also won't find recipes using a crazy long list of ingredients, or obscure, hard-to-find ones like some other books out there.

I've tried to work with recipes that use ingredients you probably already have in your kitchen. So you'll find straightforward, delicious recipes for food you already love, like:

-Lip Smacking BBQ Buffalo Chicken Wings

-Satisfying Baked Hamburger Casserole with Cheese

-Creamy Fettuccine Alfredo with Almond Crusted Chicken

-Delectable Double Chocolate Brownies

But since variety is also the spice of life I've sprinkled in some unique recipes to stretch your palette (and meal options) like:

-Heart Healthy Almond Crusted Salmon

-Savory Curry Chicken

If you have a multitude of food allergies and are on a strict diet some of these recipes will need substitutions to fit within your personal restrictions. But they should still be delicious, and I believe his book has something for everyone looking to harness the power of almond flour.

Here's to *your* better health!

Paula Sutten

What is Almond Flour?

Almond flour can also be called almond meal, and is generally made with ground blanched almonds (no skins). Almond meal can be made with either ground blanched or whole almonds, although I recommend blanched. The texture and consistency is different than wheat flour and more like corn meal (note: there can be consistency variations among the different store bought versions, please see the *Shopping Resources* at the end, if interested).

Benefits of Almond Flour & Almonds

Almond flour continues to grow in popularity, particularly for anything that requires baking in an oven. Almonds have high levels of monounsaturated fats; the same kind of healthy fats found in olive oil, and appear to decrease after-meal rises in blood sugar and insulin. It's also low in sugars, low in carbohydrates and has been linked to studies by the Nurses' Health Study to potentially reduce the risk of heart disease.

Other benefits of roughly 1 ounce of almonds are reported to include:

-Up to 35% of your daily allowance for Vitamin E

-Calcium equivalent of ¼ cup of milk

-Zinc to help your immune system

-Healthy source of fiber

-Magnesium, which can help reduce blood pressure

If that alone isn't impressive almonds have also been linked to reduced risk of diabetes, heart disease and weight gain!

Concerns with Almond Flour

Nuts (or to be exact, drupes) like almonds are a common form of food allergies, and could be potentially fatal for someone with a severe allergy to them. You must *always* share information with any guests when serving food prepared with almond flour, no exceptions.

Breakfast Recipes

Breakfast is said to be the most important meal of the day, so you want to get a good start. Here are some classics along with some other baked items you can enjoy in the morning, or just about any time of the day.

Waffles with Cinnamon

Prep Time: 10 minutes

Cook Time: 10 minutes

Serves: 6

Ingredients

1 cup blanched almond flour

A pinch of salt

1 tsp of baking soda

4 eggs

1/4 cup honey

1 tsp vanilla extract

Cooking spray

1/8-1/4 tsp cinnamon, depending on your taste preference

Instructions

1. Preheat waffle iron and grease it with a cooking spray.

2. Mix almond flour, salt, and baking soda together in a bowl.

3. In a separate bowl, mix together eggs, honey, and vanilla extract.

4. Add the dry ingredients with the wet ingredients, and mix well together.

5. Pour batter into the waffle iron. Cook until golden brown.

6. Top waffles with butter, maple syrup (or brown rice syrup, for a healthier option), and some fresh fruits if you like.

Golden Blueberry Muffins

Prep Time: 5 minutes
Cook Time: 25 minutes
Serves: 12

Ingredients

2 cups blanched almond flour
2 eggs
2 egg whites
1/4 cup honey or maple syrup
1/2 tsp baking soda
1 tbsp apple cider vinegar
1/4 tsp salt
1 tsp vanilla extract
2 tbsp olive oil
1 cup blueberries

Instructions

1. Preheat oven to 350°F. Line 12 cups in a standard 12-cup muffin tin with paper or foil liners, or spray muffin tin with cooking spray.

2. Mix all of the ingredients except the blueberries in a food processor or mixer. Blend until smooth.

3. Fold blueberries into the batter with a wooden spoon.

4. Pour the batter into muffin tin, filling it three-quarters of the way full.

5. Bake for 20-25 minutes, or until you insert a toothpick, it comes out clean, and they're golden brown.

6. Let them cool in the pan for 5 minutes before transferring them onto a wire rack to cool completely.

Fluffy Buttermilk Pancakes

Prep Time: 5 minutes

Cook Time: 5 minutes

Serves: 4

Ingredients

1 1/2 cups blanched almond flour

1/2 tsp baking soda

1/4 tsp sea salt

3 large eggs, room temperature

1/4 cup buttermilk

1 tbsp butter or coconut oil, melted

1 tbsp pure maple syrup

1 tsp pure vanilla extract

Instructions

1. Mix almond flour, baking soda, and sea salt in one bowl.

2. Add the eggs, buttermilk, and vanilla extract. Add the buttermilk slowly to reach the desired consistency of the batter.

3. Heat butter or coconut oil over medium heat; drop a large spoonful of batter into the skillet or a griddle.

4. Cook all pancakes for approximately 2-3 minutes per side or until bubbles form and both sides are golden brown. Repeat with remaining batter.

5. Top pancakes with butter, maple syrup (or brown rice syrup, for a healthy option), and some fresh fruits if you like.

Buttery Butter Biscuits

Prep Time: 5 minutes

Cook Time: 12 minutes

Serves: 6

Ingredients

2 1/2 cups of blanched almond flour

1/2 tsp of salt

1/2 tsp of baking soda

A pinch of cinnamon

1/4 cup of unsalted butter, cold

2 eggs

1 tbsp of honey

Instructions

1. Mix almond flour, baking soda, cinnamon, and salt together in a medium-sized bowl.

2. Add cold butter and, using a pastry cutter or fork, mix until crumbly.

3. In a small bowl, whisk the eggs with a fork until they are slightly frothy, about 30 seconds. Blend the eggs in with the almond flour mixture until combined.

4. Roll the dough into a ball, and place in the freezer for about 10 minutes.

5. Preheat oven to 350°F. Grease cookie sheet with cooking spray.

6. Place the dough ball in between two pieces of parchment paper, and roll it to 1-inch thickness. Cut out biscuits with a

cookie cutter, or take a bit of dough and roll it in your hands, then flatten and shape it into biscuits with a thickness of 1 inch.

7. Place biscuits on the cookie sheet and bake in the oven. Bake for 12 minutes or until you can insert a toothpick, and it comes out clean.

8. Serve with butter, or topped with gluten-free sausage gravy if you prefer.

Tasty Oatmeal Raisin Bars

Prep Time: 20 minutes
Cook Time: 20-30 minutes
Serves: 15 bars

Ingredients

11/2 cups of rolled oats
11/2 cups of blanched almond flour
1/2 tsp of salt
1/2 tsp of baking soda
1 tbsp cinnamon
2 tbsp milled golden flaxseed or wheat germ
1/2 cup of honey
1/2 cup of coconut oil or butter, melted
1 egg, beaten
1 tbsp of vanilla
11/2 to 2 cups of raisins, a combo of dried fruits and nuts or chocolate chips

Instructions

1. Preheat oven to 350°F. Grease a 13x9-inch pan with cooking oil or butter.

2. In a large bowl, mix together rolled oats, almond flour, salt, baking soda, cinnamon, and milled golden flaxseed or wheat germ.

3. Make a well in the center of the mix, pour in honey, coconut oil or butter, egg, and vanilla. Mix well using your hands.

4. Put the mixture in the prepared pan, and press it evenly.

5. Bake for 20-30 minutes or until you can insert a toothpick, and it comes out clean.

6. Cool for 5 minutes, and then cut into bars while they are still warm. It will be difficult to cut if you allow the bars to cool completely before cutting.

Cinnamon Vanilla Banana Bread

Prep Time: 15 minutes

Cook Time: 50 minutes

Serves: 12

Ingredients

2 1/2 cups blanched almond flour

1 1/2 tsp ground cinnamon

1/4 tsp ground nutmeg

1/2 tsp sea salt

1 tsp baking soda

3 eggs

1/2 cup honey

1/4 cup whole milk yogurt

2-3 very ripe bananas, mashed

1 tsp vanilla extract

1/4 cup chopped walnuts

Instructions

1. Preheat oven to 350°F. Grease a large bread pan with cooking oil or butter.

2. In a large bowl, mix together the almond flour, cinnamon, nutmeg, sea salt, and baking soda.

3. In a separate bowl, whisk the eggs using an electric mixer or hand blender.

4. Add the honey, whole milk yogurt, bananas, and vanilla extract until well combined.

5. Add the dry ingredients into the mixture one cup at a time, making sure that it is blended well after each addition.

6. Fold in the chopped walnuts using a wooden spoon.

7. Pour the batter into the large bread pan.

8. Bake in the oven for 50 minutes, until the center is firm or a toothpick is inserted and comes out clean.

9. Remove from the oven and transfer onto a wire rack to cool completely.

10. Slice the loaf, and enjoy it with butter and coffee (optional).

Moist Pumpkin Spice Bread

Prep Time: 10 minutes
Cook Time: 35 minutes
Serves: 12

Ingredients

1 cup blanched almond flour
1/4 tsp sea salt
1/2 tsp baking soda
2 tbsp cinnamon
2 tsp nutmeg
1 tsp cloves
1 tsp ginger
1 tsp Allspice (or substitute)
1/2 cup roasted pumpkin or winter squash, mashed
3 eggs
3 tbsp honey
1/4 tsp Stevia drops (optional – to make slightly sweeter)

Instructions

1. Preheat oven to 350°F. Grease 5x9-inch bread pan or two mini bread pans with cooking oil or butter.

2. In a medium bowl, mix almond flour, sea salt, baking soda, cinnamon, nutmeg, cloves, ginger, and Allspice together until well-blended.

3. In a separate bowl, mix pumpkin or winter squash, eggs, honey, and Stevia drops using an electric mixer or hand blender until smooth.

4. Add the dry ingredients into the mixture one cup at a time, making sure that it is blended well after each addition.

5. Pour batter into the bread pan or two mini bread pans.

6. Bake in the oven for 35 minutes, until the center is firm or until a toothpick is inserted and comes out clean.

7. Remove from the oven, and transfer onto a wire rack to cool completely.

Lunch Recipes

Lunch (or in some parts of the country, Dinner) is an important midday meal that was 'institutionalised' in England, and shouldn't be missed. You'll find some great recipes on the following pages for something light, like a soup, or more satisfying like burgers. Enjoy!

Great Green Bean and Almond Soup

Prep Time: 15 minutes

Cook Time: 40 minutes

Serves: 6

Ingredients

3 tbsp olive oil

2 onions, peeled and chopped

1 garlic clove, peeled and smashed

3 carrots, peeled and sliced

500 grams (2-3 cups) green beans

4 cups homemade vegetable stock or water

1 cup blanched almond flour

Instructions

1. Heat the olive oil in a medium sized pot.

2. Add the onions, garlic, and carrots, and cook over medium heat, stirring every now and then, until softened and very lightly golden. In the meantime, trim the green beans, and rinse them well.

3. Add the green beans to the pot, season with salt and pepper, and cook for five minutes, stirring from time to time.

4. Pour in the stock or water and bring to a simmer. Cover and cook for 30 minutes, until all the vegetables are soft.

5. In the meantime, pour the almond flour in a dry skillet. Set over medium-high heat, and toast for about two minutes, stirring constantly and watching closely until golden.

6. Set the almond flour aside in a bowl to prevent over-toasting.

7. When the vegetables are soft, add the almond flour to the pot, and stir well.

8. Remove from heat, and let cool slightly.

9. Purée the soup using a blender until completely smooth.

10. Taste and adjust the seasoning. Serve while warm.

Crispy Homemade Pizza Crust

Prep Time: 10 minutes

Cook Time: 90 minutes

Serves: 6

Ingredients

1 tbsp yeast

1 tbsp honey

1/4 cup warm water

3/4 cup blanched almond flour

3/4 cup tapioca starch or corn starch

3/4 tsp sea salt

1 tbsp olive oil or butter

1 tbsp egg white (less than one egg)

1 1/2 teaspoons apple cider vinegar

Instructions

1. In a warm bowl, whisk yeast, honey, and warm water using an electric mixer or hand blender. Let it sit for five minutes, until it gets foamy and active.

2. In a small bowl, add olive oil, apple cider vinegar, and egg white for the wet ingredients.

3. In another separate bowl, add the almond flour, tapioca or corn starch, and sea salt.

4. Once the yeast is foamy, add the wet and dry ingredients, and whisk it for 30 seconds on medium-high, making sure that everything is blended together.

5. Scrape the bowl using a rubber spatula to gather the dough together. Cover it with a tea towel, and set it in a place that is room temperature. Let it rise for an hour and fifteen minutes.

6. Check if the dough has risen; when this happens, turn on your oven to 350°F.

7. Lightly oil a parchment paper, and transfer the dough there.

8. With oiled hands, gently knead the dough, and flatten it in a 10–inch circle.

9. Carefully transfer the parchment paper with the dough onto a pizza stone or sheet pan.

10. Bake it on the lower part of the oven for eight minutes, or until you see the edges turned light brown.

11. Add desired toppings, and bake it for another five minutes.

12. Let it cool for one minute before slicing.

Tasty Lean Beef Hamburgers

Prep Time: 20 minutes

Cook Time: 10 minutes

Serves: 5

Ingredients

1 lb lean ground beef

2 eggs

1/4 yellow onion

1 garlic clove

1/2 cup of blanched almond flour

1/2 tsp of sea salt

1/4 tsp of pepper

Olive oil for brushing

Instructions

1. Start and heat a gas grill to high, or heat coals in a charcoal grill until they glow bright orange and ash over.

2. Chop your onion and garlic clove. Place in mixing bowl.

3. Add the ground beef, eggs, almond flour, sea salt, and pepper to the same mixing bowl.

4. Using your hands, mix all of these ingredients together. Make sure no spices are left out in the bottom of the bowl.

5. Make patties (palm-size) with the mixture, and place them on a baking sheet.

6. Brush the burgers with olive oil. Grill the burgers until golden brown and slightly charred on the first side, about 3 minutes.

7. Cook beef burgers until golden brown and slightly charred on the second side, about 4 minutes for medium-rare or 3 minutes if topping with cheese.

8. You can also cook them longer until they reach the desired degree of doneness, just make sure they're cooked enough to be safe.

9. Serve on gluten-free buns, or better yet, on a bed of crisp lettuce and apply favorite toppings.

Juicy Turkey Burgers

Prep Time: 15 minutes

Cook Time: 10 minutes

Serves: 5

Ingredients

1 tbsp extra-virgin olive oil, additional for frying

1 medium onion, finely chopped

1 lb of high quality ground turkey

1/3 cup blanched almond flour

2 eggs, beaten

Handful of fresh parsley or 1 tbsp of dried parsley

Pinch of salt and pepper

Instructions

1. In a skillet, heat olive oil over the medium heat setting and sauté the onion until soft and golden.

2. In a large bowl, add the turkey, almond flour, cooled onions, two beaten eggs, parsley, and salt.

3. Coat your hands with oil, and mix the ingredients gently and completely. If the mixture is really sticky, add a little more almond flour.

4. When ingredients are mixed well shape into round burger patties.

5. In a medium pan, heat olive oil, and cook the patties over medium heat until browned, about five minutes on the first side.

6. Flip the burgers, and cover the pan. Reduce the heat just a notch, and continue to cook for another five minutes. This will steam them and keep them moist until the juices run clear.

7. Serve on gluten-free buns, or better yet, on a bed of crisp lettuce and apply your favorite toppings.

Lip Smacking BBQ Buffalo Chicken Wings

Prep Time: 20 minutes

Cook Time: 30 minutes

Serves: 16

Ingredients

1 lb chicken wings

1/2 cup blanched almond flour

1 tbsp Ranch seasoning, with an additional 1 tbsp

1 egg, beaten

1 tbsp duck fat or preferred cooking fat for frying

2 tbsp tomato paste

2–3 tbsp hot sauce, depending on preferred hotness

2 tbsp coconut milk

Instructions

1. Preheat oven to 350°F. Grease with oil, or place a parchment paper on a baking sheet.

2. Mix together the almond flour and ranch seasoning in a small bowl. In a separate bowl, put in the beaten egg.

3. Dip each chicken wing in egg, then almond flour mixture, and set aside on a plate.

4. In a frying pan on medium heat, add the duck fat.

5. Place the chicken wings into the pan, and fry them on each side for about ten minutes total. Keep an eye on them so they don't burn!

6. Let them cool. Mix together the tomato paste, hot sauce, coconut milk, and remaining ranch seasoning in another small bowl.

7. Dip each wing into the sauce, and coat it well.

8. Bake for ten minutes, then flip the wings, and bake for another 5–10 minutes.

9. Remove from the oven and enjoy with celery, Ranch dressing, or if a purist, Blue Cheese dressing.

Chicken Tenders with Homemade Honey Mustard Sauce

Prep Time: 15 minutes
Cook Time: 20 minutes
Serves: 12

Ingredients

1 lb boneless, skinless chicken breasts
1 cup blanched almond flour
1 tbsp paprika
1/2 tsp garlic powder
1 tsp cumin
1 tsp cayenne pepper
1 tsp black pepper
1 tsp sea salt
2 eggs, lightly beaten
Cooking spray

Instructions

1. Preheat oven to 350°F. Grease with cooking spray, or place a parchment paper on a baking sheet.

2. Slice chicken breasts into long strips, 1-2–inches wide.

3. In a medium bowl, mix together almond meal, paprika, garlic, cumin, cayenne pepper, black pepper, and sea salt until well-blended.

4. Dip each piece of chicken in beaten egg, and then coat with almond spice mixture. Place it on the baking sheet.

5. Bake for ten minutes; then flip the tenders and bake for another ten minutes or until they are golden brown.

6. Remove from the oven, and serve with a honey mustard dip.

Honey Mustard Sauce

Prep Time: 2 minutes
Cook Time: 2 minutes

Ingredients

1/2 cup of mayonnaise
1/4 cup mustard or Dijon mustard
1/4 cup honey
1/2 tsp salt
1/2 tsp pepper

Instructions

1. Mix all ingredients in a blender or with a whisk until well-blended and smooth.

2. Serve on the side with the chicken tenders for a satisfying dipping sauce.

Crispy Fish Sticks with Homemade Tartar Sauce

Prep Time: 15 minutes

Cook Time: 20 minutes

Serves: 20

Ingredients

1 lb cod fish or any preferred white fish

2 eggs, beaten

4 tbsp blanched almond flour

5 tbsp gluten-free bread crumbs

1 tsp garlic powder

1 tsp parsley flakes

Sea salt and pepper to taste

Instructions

1. Preheat oven to 350°F. Grease with oil, or place a parchment paper on a baking sheet.

2. In a medium bowl, combine the almond flour, bread crumbs, garlic powder, parsley flakes, sea salt, and pepper. Set aside.

3. Slice fish into long strips, 4 inches long and 1 inch wide.

4. Dip each fish piece into the beaten eggs, and then coat with almond spice mixture. Place it on the baking sheet.

5. Bake for 20 minutes or until lightly browned and fish feels firm to touch.

6. Remove from the oven, and serve with lemon wedges and tartar sauce.

Tartar Sauce

Prep Time: 2 minutes
Cook Time: 2 minutes

Ingredients

1 cup mayonnaise
1/2 tbsp lemon juice or apple cider vinegar
1 tbsp minced onion
1/4 tsp sea salt
1/4 tsp garlic powder
1/2 tsp dried dill
Dash of fresh parsley (optional)

Instructions

1. Mix all ingredients together until well-combined.

2. Store in the refrigerator for 30 minutes or more before serving with the fish sticks.

Dinner Recipes

Dinner is considered by many to be the most important meal of the day, and also called Supper by some. Since it is such key meal, and the one we struggle the most figuring out, I've included a variety of recipes to pick from. Dig in!

Satisfying Baked Hamburger Casserole with Cheese

Prep Time: 20 minutes

Cook Time: 30 minutes

Serves: 8

Ingredients

1 (12 oz) pkg. gluten-free lasagna noodles

1 1/2 lbs ground beef

2 tbsp fresh parsley, chopped

3/4 cup grated Parmesan cheese

1/2 cup blanched almond flour

2 eggs

1 tsp sea salt

1/4 tsp ground black pepper

1/4 tsp minced garlic

1/2 cup minced onion

1/4 tsp dried oregano

3 (8 oz) cans tomato sauce

1 (8 oz) pkg. cream cheese, softened

1/2 cup of sour cream

1/4 cup sliced green onion

1/4 cup grated Mozzarella cheese

Bacon fat or any other fat for frying

Instructions

1. Preheat oven to 350°F. Prepare 11x7x1-½-inch baking dish.

2. In a large pot, boil water and add some salt. Cook pasta until its al dente. Drain and set aside.

3. In a large bowl, combine ground beef, parsley, Parmesan cheese, almond flour, eggs, sea salt, black pepper, garlic, onion, and oregano until well-blended.

4. In a medium pan, heat bacon fat, and cook the mixture until browned. Add the tomato sauce, and mix well. Remove from heat.

5. In a medium bowl, whisk the cream cheese, sour cream, and green onion together until smooth and well-combined.

6. To assemble in a baking dish, spread the bottom with half of the pasta, and then pour in half of the meat sauce and all of the cheese sauce.

7. Cover the remaining pasta; then pour in the remaining meat sauce. Top it with grated Mozzarella cheese.

8. Bake in the oven for 30 minutes. Remove and let it cool for ten minutes before serving with gluten-free garlic bread (optional).

Hearty Baked Turkey Meatloaf

Prep Time: 30 minutes

Cook Time: 90 minutes

Serves: 10

Ingredients

3 cups yellow onions, chopped

2 tbsp extra virgin olive oil

2 tsp sea salt

1 tsp freshly ground black pepper

1 tsp fresh thyme leaves or 1/2 tsp dried

1/3 cup Worcestershire sauce

3/4 cup chicken stock

1 1/2 tsp tomato paste

5 lbs ground turkey

1 1/2 cups blanched almond flour

3 large eggs, beaten

3/4 cup ketchup, tomato sauce or BBQ sauce

Instructions

1. Preheat oven to 350°F.

2. In a large skillet over medium-low heat, add extra virgin olive oil.

3. Add onions, salt, pepper, and thyme until the onions are translucent but not browned.

4. Add the Worcestershire sauce, chicken stock, and tomato paste. Remove from heat and set aside to cool at room temperature.

5. In a large bowl, combine turkey, almond flour, eggs, and cooled onion mixture together. Use your hands or a wooden mixing spoon to blend mixture well.

6. Transfer mixture onto a work surface and form into a rectangular loaf.

7. Place meatloaf on a loaf pan or meatloaf pan. Brush the top and sides of the meatloaf with ketchup, tomato sauce, or barbeque sauce.

8. Bake meatloaf in the oven, and put it on the middle rack for 1 1/2 hours. Place a pan of hot water on a lower rack to prevent the loaf from cracking.

9. Remove from oven and allow it to cool for ten minutes before slicing. Add more of the ketchup, tomato sauce, or BBQ sauce as desired. Serve while it is hot.

Almond and Cheesy Parmesan Baked Fish

Prep Time: 10 minutes

Cook Time: 25 minutes

Serves: 4

Ingredients

4 tilapia filets or any white fish, thawed if frozen

1/4 cup melted butter

1/3 cup blanched almond flour

2 tbsp finely grated parmesan or Asiago cheese

1/2 tsp garlic powder

1/4 tsp ground black pepper

1/4 tsp sea salt

Instructions

1. Preheat oven to 350°F. Grease a baking dish with cooking oil or butter.

2. In a flat bowl, mix the almond flour, parmesan or Asiago cheese, garlic powder, black pepper, and sea salt together until well-blended.

3. Dip each fish in melted butter, and coat it in the almond mixture evenly, making sure that both sides are coated well. Place the fish into the baking dish.

4. Bake it in the oven for 25 minutes, until fish is firm to the touch and crust is golden brown.

5. Remove from the oven, and let it cool for five minutes. Serve with tartar sauce and lemon wedges on the side.

Tantalizing Turkey Meatballs

Prep Time: 10 minutes
Cook Time: 20 minutes
Serves: 20

Ingredients

2 lbs ground turkey
2 eggs
1 small red bell pepper, chopped
1 small green bell pepper, chopped
1/2 medium-sized purple onion, chopped
3 garlic cloves, finely diced
1/4 cup blanched almond flour
1 tsp sea salt
1 tsp black pepper
1 tsp dried parsley
Coconut or olive oil for frying

Instructions

1. In a skillet under medium heat, add coconut oil.

2. Add onion, and cook it until soft and translucent. Add the red and green bell peppers.

3. Add the garlic and sauté. Remove the pan from the heat, and pour the mixture in a bowl. Set aside, and let it cool.

4. In a separate bowl, combine the turkey, eggs, sea salt, black pepper, almond flour and the cooled onion, pepper, and garlic mixture.

5. Place parchment paper on a sheet. Form mixture into 1 1/2–inch sized balls, and put it on the parchment paper.

6. Place the skillet under medium heat, and melt the coconut oil or heat the olive oil. Place the meatballs in the skillet, and cover them with a lid. Let it cook for about four minutes or until the bottom gets golden brown.

7. Turn the meatballs to the other side, and let them cook for another four minutes or until they get golden brown. Be sure to put the lid back again.

8. Repeat the process until all of the meatballs are cooked.

9. Serve the meatballs on top of gluten-free pasta, mixed greens, or on a bed of cauliflower mash.

Savory Curry Chicken

Prep Time: 10 minutes

Cook Time: 30 minutes

Serves: 4

Ingredients

1 lb of boneless and skinless chicken thighs, diced up into cubes

4 cloves of garlic, peeled and finely chopped

1 inch of fresh ginger root, peeled and finely grated

1 small red chilli, to taste and finely chopped (optional)

Juice of half of a lemon

1/2 cup of flaked or slivered almonds

2 onions, peeled and sliced

1 cinnamon stick

4 cardamom pods, crushed slightly with the top of a knife handle

3 whole cloves

1 tsp of cumin powder

1 tsp of coriander powder

1 tsp of turmeric powder

1/3 cup blanched almond flour

Pinch of sea salt and black pepper for seasoning

1/4 cup currants or sultanas (optional)

10 oz of natural yoghurt

1/2 cup of fresh or frozen peas

Coriander leaves, to serve

Instructions

1. In a large bowl, mix the chicken, ginger, garlic, red chilli, and lemon juice. Marinade for an hour or so.

2. In a medium fry pan, toast the slivered or flaked almonds over a low heat and set aside.

3. In a wok or pan, melt coconut oil or ghee over a low to medium heat, and cook the onion until it starts to soften.

4. Add the cinnamon stick, cardamom pods, and cloves, and cook for a few minutes, until you can smell them.

5. Then add cumin, coriander, turmeric powders, and almond flour.

6. Mix well together, add the chicken to the pan, and stir gently until the chicken starts to turn opaque. Season with a good pinch of sea salt and black pepper.

7. Next, add the yoghurt and currants or sultanas, and mix well.

8. Cover and simmer slowly for 20-30 minutes, stirring occasionally, making sure it doesn't stick to the bottom of the pan.

9. Just before serving, stir in the peas and top with coriander.

10. Serve with brown or basmati rice and some steamed vegetables on the side.

Heart Healthy Almond Crusted Salmon

Prep Time: 10 minutes

Cook Time: 15 minutes

Serves: 4

Ingredients

1/4 cup blanched almond flour

1/4 cup gluten-free bread crumbs

1/4 tsp ground coriander

1/8 tsp ground cumin

4 (6-oz) salmon fillets, skin on about 1-inch thick

2 tsp lemon juice

1/2 tsp kosher salt

1/4 tsp freshly ground black pepper

Sprig of fresh cilantro

Lemon wedges

Instructions

1. Preheat oven to 350°F. Grease a broiler pan with cooking oil or butter.

2. In a medium bowl, combine almond flour, bread crumbs, ground coriander, and ground cumin, mixing it well. Set aside.

3. Brush salmon with lemon juice on both sides, and season with salt and pepper.

4. Coat the salmon evenly, and place it skin-side down on the broiler pan. Sprinkle the remaining crumb mixture on the fish.

5. Bake in the oven for fifteen minutes or until salmon flakes easily with a fork. You can also cook it longer until the desired doneness.

6. Remove from the oven and serve with a sprig of fresh cilantro on top and a lemon wedge at the side for each fish.

(Oven-Fried) Fried Chicken

Prep Time: 30 minutes

Cook Time: 90 minutes

Serves: 8

Ingredients

1 (4 to 5 lb) chicken, cut up into 8 pieces

1 1/2 cup almond meal

3/4 cup blanched almond flour

1 1/2 tbsp kosher salt

1 tsp black pepper

1/2 tsp cayenne pepper

1 1/2 tsp paprika

1/2 tsp dried oregano

1/2 tsp garlic powder

2 eggs

1/8 cup unsweetened, plain almond milk

Cooking spray

Instructions

1. Preheat oven to 350°F. Prepare baking sheet by lining it with foil and putting a cooking rack on top of it. Spray the rack generously with the cooking spray.

2. In a medium bowl, mix almond meal and almond flour together. Add kosher salt, black pepper, cayenne pepper, paprika, oregano, and garlic powder until well-blended.

3. In a flat bowl, combine eggs and almond milk together. Mix well.

4. Dip a piece of chicken into the egg mixture. Then coat the chicken with the almond mixture evenly until well-coated. Place the chicken on the rack.

5. Repeat the process to all chicken pieces. Spray them with the cooking spray.

6. Put the chickens in the oven, and bake them for 1 1/2 hours, until the chicken is golden brown.

7. Remove from the oven, and cool them for ten minutes before serving. Optionally serve with gravy on the side.

Creamy Fettuccine Alfredo with Almond Crusted Chicken

Prep Time: 30 minutes

Cook Time: 35 minutes

Serves: 6

Ingredients

1 pkg. of gluten-free fettuccini pasta

2 tbsp olive oil or butter, additional for cooking

1/4 cup oat flour

1 cup shaved Parmesan cheese

2 cups fresh milk

1/2 cup blanched almond flour

1/2 cup Mozzarella cheese

1 lb chicken breast, skinless and sliced

1 tsp black pepper

1 tsp paprika

Kosher salt to taste (optional)

Instructions

1. In a medium pot, cook pasta in boiling water with olive oil and kosher salt. Cook according to package directions, until al dente. Drain and set aside.

2. In a saucepan on medium heat, add olive oil or butter; then add oat flour, whisking to combine. Toast the flour mixture, creating a roux that's lightly browned.

3. Whisk in the milk until it reaches a smooth consistency, and allow the mixture to simmer.

4. Add grated parmesan to simmering sauce, whisking to combine well.

5. In a small bowl, mix together almond flour, salt, pepper, and paprika. Take chicken breast pieces and toss them in the mixture, fully coating them.

6. In a hot skillet with olive oil or butter, cook the coated chicken breasts.

7. To serve, put down a layer of hot pasta and top with chicken and cheese sauce. Sprinkle with mozzarella for an extra cheesy taste.

Dessert Recipes

I saved the best for last...desserts!

Classic Chocolate Chip Cookies

Prep Time: 10 minutes

Cook Time: 15 minutes

Serves: 12 cookies

Ingredients

1 1/2 cups blanched almond flour

1/4 cup butter or coconut oil (room temperature)

1/4 cup sugar

1 egg

1/4 tsp salt

1/2 tsp vanilla extract

1/4 tsp baking soda

1/4 cup chocolate chips

1/4 cup chopped nuts, optional

Instructions

1. Preheat oven to 350°F. Line a baking sheet with parchment paper.

2. In a larger bowl, cream together coconut oil or butter and sugar using an electric mixer or hand blender.

3. Gradually add egg and vanilla extract into the mixture.

4. Mix in the baking soda and salt.

5. Add almond flour into the mixture one cup at a time, making sure that it is mixed well after each addition.

6. Fold chocolate chips and nuts using a wooden spoon.

7. Roll the dough into 1-inch balls, and press them down gently onto the baking sheet.

8. Bake for 12-15 minutes, until the dough rises and the edges are lightly browned.

9. Remove the cookies from the oven, and let them cool completely before enjoying.

Scrumptious Apple Pie

Prep Time: 10 minutes

Cook Time: 45 minutes

Serves: 8

Ingredients

Crust

2 1/2 cups blanched almond flour

1/4 tsp sea salt

1/2 cup coconut oil or butter, melted

1 tsp sugar

1 cup (2 sticks) chilled unsalted butter, cut into pieces

1/4 to 1/2 cup ice water

Filling

2 tbsp blanched almond flour

6-8 Granny Smith apples, peeled, cored, and sliced

3/4 cup sugar, plus additional for pie top

1 lemon, zest finely grated and juiced

1 1/2 tsp cinnamon

1/2 tsp nutmeg

Pinch ground cloves

2 tbsp unsalted butter

1 large egg, beaten

Instructions

Crust

1. Place the flour, salt, and sugar in the bowl of a food processor, and process for a few seconds to combine.

2. Add the butter, and process until the mixture resembles coarse meal, about 10 seconds.

3. With the machine running, add the ice water in a slow, steady stream through the feed tube, just until the dough holds together. Do not process for more than 30 seconds.

4. Turn the dough out onto a work surface. Divide in two. Place each half onto a sheet of plastic wrap. Flatten, and form two discs.

5. Wrap and refrigerate for at least one hour before using.

Filling
1. Heat oven to 375°F. On a lightly floured surface, roll out dough into two 1/8-inch-thick circles to a diameter slightly larger than that of an 11-inch plate.

2. Press one pastry circle into the pie plate. Place the other circle onto waxed paper, and cover with plastic wrap. Chill all pastry until firm, about 30 minutes.

3. In a large bowl, combine apples, sugar, lemon zest, lemon juice, cinnamon, nutmeg, cloves, and almond flour. Mix well.

4. Spoon apples into pie pan. Dot with butter, and cover with remaining pastry circle.

5. Cut several steam vents across the top. Seal by crimping edges by a fork.

6. Brush the top with beaten egg, and sprinkle with additional sugar.

7. Bake until crust is brown and juices are bubbling, about 45 minutes. Let it cool on a wire rack.

8. Serve with a scoop of vanilla ice cream on top, and sprig of mint for presentation (optional).

Delectable Double Chocolate Brownies

Prep Time: 10 minutes

Cook Time: 20 minutes

Serves: 12 brownies

Ingredients

2 1/2 cups blanched almond flour

1 tsp baking soda

1/2 cup raw cacao (or cocoa powder)

1/2 tsp sea salt

1/3 cup honey

2 large eggs

1/4 cup butter or coconut oil, melted

2 tsp vanilla extract

2 tbsp almond milk

3/4 cup semi-sweet chocolate chips

Instructions

1. Preheat oven to 350°F. Grease an 8x8-inch pan with cooking oil or butter.

2. In a large bowl, mix together the almond flour, baking soda, raw cacao or cocoa powder, and sea salt until well blended.

3. In a separate bowl, whisk the butter or coconut oil until smooth in an electric mixer or by using a hand blender.

4. Add the eggs, honey, vanilla extract, and almond milk.

5. Mix the dry ingredients into the mixture one cup at a time, making sure that it is blended well after each addition.

6. Fold the chocolate chips into the batter using a wooden spoon.

7. Pour the batter into the 8x8-inch pan.

8. Bake in the oven for 20 minutes until the center sets, or until a toothpick is inserted and comes out clean.

9. Let it cool for 10-15 minutes before cutting it into bars.

10. Enjoy while warm, and store refrigerated up to five days.

Perfect Peanut Butter Cookies

Prep Time: 10 minutes

Cook Time: 15 minutes

Serves: 12

Ingredients

1 cup peanut butter

1/2 cup butter, softened

3/4 cup honey

2 eggs

11/2 cup blanched almond flour

1/2 tsp baking soda

1/4 tsp salt

1/4 tsp cinnamon

Instructions

1. Preheat oven to 350°F. Line a baking sheet with parchment paper.

2. In a larger bowl, cream together peanut butter, butter, and honey using an electric mixer or hand blender.

3. Gradually add an egg, one at a time, making sure that it is well blended before adding in the next one.

4. Mix in the baking soda, salt, and cinnamon.

5. Add almond flour into the mixture one cup at a time, making sure that it is mixed well after each addition.

6. Roll the dough into 1-inch balls, and press them down gently onto the baking sheet.

7. Bake for 12-15 minutes until the dough rises, and the edges are lightly browned.

8. Remove the cookies from the oven, let them cool to the touch, and enjoy warm.

Mouth-Watering Peach Crisp

Prep Time: 15 minutes

Cook Time: 40 minutes

Serves: 6

Ingredients

1 pound peaches (2-3 medium) cut into 1/2-inch dice (about 4 cups)

1/2 tsp lemon zest

1/2 tbsp lemon juice

1/3 cup blanched almond flour

4 dried dates, pitted

1/4 tsp cinnamon

1/8 tsp nutmeg

1/8 tsp salt

1 tbsp butter

1/4 cup sliced almonds

Instructions

1. Preheat oven to 350°F. Grease an 8-inch square pan with cooking oil or butter.

2. In a medium bowl, mix the peaches, lemon zest, and lemon juice with a wooden spoon. Allow to rest at room temperature while you prepare the topping.

3. Place the almond flour, dates, cinnamon, nutmeg, and salt in a food processor. Press Pulse until combined.

4. Add the butter. Pulse again about 10 times, and then process on high for 5-10 seconds until there are no lumps.

5. Transfer the mixture into a bowl and fold in the almond slices.

6. Pour the peach mixture into the pan, pressing it gently into place with the back of a wooden spoon.

7. Sprinkle the almond topping over the fruit, and lightly press it into the fruit with the back of the spoon.

8. Cover the crisp lightly with foil and bake for 30 minutes. Remove foil and bake 5-10 minutes more, until browned.

9. Serve while warm.

Awesome Almond Brownies

Prep Time: 10 minutes

Cook Time: 20 minutes

Serves: 9

Ingredients

2 tbsp butter, softened

1/2 cup sugar

1 egg

1/4 cup unsweetened almond milk

1 teaspoon vanilla extract

1 cup blanched almond flour

1/4 cup unsweetened cocoa powder

1/8 tsp sea salt

1 tsp baking powder

1/4 cup chopped whole natural almonds

1/4 cup dark chocolate chips

More almonds for garnish

Instructions

1. Preheat oven to 350°F. Grease 8x8-inch pan with cooking oil or butter, or spray it with cooking spray.

2. In a large bowl, whisk butter and sugar together using an electric mixer or hand blender.

3. Add almond milk and vanilla extract.

4. In a separate bowl, mix the almond flour, cocoa powder, sea salt, and baking powder until well blended.

5. Add the dry ingredients into the mixture one cup at a time, making sure that it is blended well after each addition.

6. Fold the almonds and chocolate chips into the mixture.

7. Pour the batter into the 8x8-inch pan.

8. Bake in the oven for 20 minutes, until the center sets or a toothpick is inserted and it comes out clean.

9. Remove from the oven. Cool for 10 minutes before cutting into bars.

10. Optionally add more chopped or toasted almonds before serving.

Conclusion

I hope you've enjoyed this book and have already tried some of the recipes.

Remember that almond flour is different, and has more of a hearty, nutty flavor compared to traditional flour. It might take a little getting used to for some recipes. Feel free to experiment and make tweaks to fit your palette, or add additional ingredients you enjoy. Life is about trying new things and making changes, so feel free to experiment.

If you'd like to email me about the recipes, or anything in general, I'm here to listen and share – Paula@kjjepublishing.com

Thanks for reading, and here's to *your* better health!

Thank You Bonus Gift

I want to say Thank You for buying my book, so I've put together a free gift for you!

More Awesome Dessert Recipes For Free

These additional recipes are the perfect complement to all the excellent recipes already in this book, and can be found at the website below:

http://www.kjjepublishing.com/almondflourbonus

Free Almond Flour & Almond Educational Resources

http://www.webmd.com/food-recipes/features/gluten-free-cooking-and-baking

http://www.ncbi.nlm.nih.gov/pubmed/11122711

http://www.whfoods.com/genpage.php?tname=foodspice&dbid=20#safetyissues

http://www.livestrong.com/article/52081-almond-flour-nutrition-information/

http://lowcarbdiets.about.com/od/lowcarbsuperfoods/a/Almonds-Health-And-Nutrition.htm

Shopping Resources

There are numerous options for store bought almond flour. Unfortunately I've not had good luck with the most common brand available, Bob's Red Mill almond flour. Besides boutique mail order options another fairly household brand is *Honeyville's blanched almond flour*. They make great almond flour, which I recommend using for the recipes in this book if possible.

For dishes that suggest using pasta I recommend the *Ronzoni* brand after trying all kinds of them. It's the closest to the real thing, in my opinion.

Glutino makes a great gluten-free bread crumb product if you're looking for a *Panko* substitute. Their other products are excellent too.

Brown rice syrup is a healthier option for pancakes and waffles, and something I enjoy. *Lundberg Organic Sweet Dreams Brown Rice Syrup* is my favorite.

Cinnamon is a common ingredient for baking, and something I use constantly (try adding it to your coffee grounds before brewing as a substitute for sugar/sugar substitutes). My current favor is *Organic Ceylon Cinnamon from Frontier Herb*.

Enjoy my book?

Please leave a review and let others know what you liked at:

http://www.amazon.com/dp/B00L87JO6A

Reviews are crucial to authors and I'd greatly appreciate it if you'd leave a quick one. Even a short sentence (or two) helps!

Warm Regards,

-Paula Sutten

Special Thanks

Books today usually aren't written solo on a Remington portable no. 3 typewriter banging away, page after page (especially recipes books)! So I'd like to extend my thanks to some people:

-Natasha Francesca Consolacion S. Cruz for her research help and support.

-Angie for collaborating and creating an excellent cover.

-Chris Robinson Brotherhood and Rich Robinson for the great music they continue to make.

-John Podlasek and his small, dedicated team at KJJE Publishing, looking forward to publishing more books with your group!

Made in the USA
Lexington, KY
29 August 2017